THE WIZARD OF OZ™ COOKBOOK

BREAKFAST IN KANSAS
DESSERT IN OZ

Sarah Key
Jennifer Newman Brazil
Vicki Wells

ABBEVILLE PRESS PUBLISHERS
New York   London   Paris

DESIGNER: Patricia Fabricant
PRODUCTION MANAGER: Matthew Pimm
COPYEDITOR: Virginia Croft

Special thanks to Tom Sabatino, Nicole and Jessica Garvey, and
Kermit Sullivan for assistance in recipe testing and development.

ALSO AVAILABLE IN THE HOLLYWOOD HOTPLATES SERIES:

The Casablanca Cookbook ★ *A Christmas Carol Cookbook*
Gone With The Wind Cookbook™ ★ *The "I Love Lucy"*™ *Cookbook*

First edition
10 9 8 7 6 5

Library of Congress Cataloging-in-Publication Data
Key, Sarah
   The Wizard of Oz cookbook : dinner in Kansas, dessert in Oz /
Sarah Key, Jennifer Newman Brazil, Vicki Wells.
        p.   cm.
   ISBN 1-55859-582-1
   1. Cookery, American—Midwestern style.   2.Wizard of Oz (Motion picture)
I. Brazil, Jennifer Newman.   II. Wells, Vicki.
III. Title
TX715.2.M53K49   1993
641.5977—dc20   93-24607

METRIC CONVERSIONS: 1 TEASPOON = 5 ML; 1 TABLESPOON = 14.8 ML.

BREAKFAST IN KANSAS

PROFESSOR MARVEL: Well—
well—well! Houseguests, huh?
DOROTHY: Oh, Toto! That's not
polite! We haven't been asked yet!

ZEKE'S HONEY BAKED HAM

ZEKE: *Soo-eee! (shooing in a wayward hog) Get in there before I make a dime bank outa ya! (pouring feed in trough) Listen kid—are you going to let that old Gulch heifer try and buffalo ya? She ain't nothing to be afraid of. Have a little courage, that's all.*

1 ham, about 6 pounds (2.7 kg), bone in
½ cup (130 g) prepared mustard
1 cup (240 g) firmly packed light brown sugar
2 cups (120 g) fresh breadcrumbs
3 tablespoons honey

Preheat oven to 350°F (180°C). Place ham in a shallow roasting pan, fat side up. Score fat with a knife. In a small bowl, stir together mustard, brown sugar, breadcrumbs, and honey. Spread mixture over top of ham. Bake for about 1 hour. Let rest for 5 minutes. Carve and serve.

SERVES 6 TO 8 PEOPLE FOR BRUNCH.

GALE FARM CHICKEN HASH

PROFESSOR MARVEL: *Ah, what's this I see? A house . . . with a picket fence and a barn with a weather vane and . . .*
DOROTHY: *That's our farm!*

8 ounces or 1½ cups (227 g) coarsely diced unpeeled small red potatoes
3 tablespoons (42 g) unsalted butter
1 whole boneless chicken breast, split
salt and freshly ground black pepper to taste
⅔ cup (70 g) finely diced onions

¾ cup (90 g) diced mushrooms
⅔ cup (160 ml) heavy cream
1¼ teaspoons Dijon mustard
few drops Worcestershire sauce
few drops Tabasco or other hot pepper sauce
2 teaspoons curry powder (optional)
1 tablespoon vegetable oil
juice of 1 lemon or 2 tablespoons sherry
minced fresh parsley
toast

Boil potatoes in a pot of salted water until just tender, about 5 minutes. Meanwhile, in a skillet, melt 2 tablespoons butter. Cook chicken breast in butter over medium heat, about 5 minutes on each side, until just cooked. Remove chicken from pan and season with salt and pepper. Set aside to cool. When cool, cut into medium dice.

Meanwhile, cook onions in pan drippings over low heat until transparent. Add mushrooms and season with salt and pepper. Cook until mushrooms exude their juices, 5 to 7 minutes. Remove mushroom and onion mixture from skillet, then clean skillet. Mix cream, mustard, Worcestershire sauce, pepper sauce, and curry powder in a small bowl. Set aside.

Heat remaining 1 tablespoon butter with vegetable oil in skillet until very hot. Add diced chicken and potatoes and sauté for 30 seconds. Add mushrooms and onions, and continue to cook over medium-high heat for 30 seconds. Add cream mixture to pan. When cream boils, add lemon juice or sherry, then cook 1 minute. Garnish with parsley and serve immediately with toast.

MAKES 4 SERVINGS.

Uncle Henry's Open-Faced Omelet

1 tablespoon corn oil
5 slices bacon, diced
1 tablespoon (14 g) unsalted butter
4 scallions, chopped
6 large eggs, lightly beaten
1½ ounces (40 g) cream cheese, cut into bits
freshly ground black pepper to taste

Preheat oven to 350°F (180°C). Coat a 10-inch (25-cm) ovenproof skillet with corn oil. Heat skillet over medium heat and cook diced bacon until crispy, stirring frequently. Drain bacon and reserve 2 tablespoons bacon drippings. Clean skillet. Add 2 tablespoons reserved bacon grease with butter to skillet. Sauté scallions over medium heat for 30 seconds. Add bacon and eggs. Stir and scrape bottom with plastic spatula or wooden spoon until eggs begin to thicken, about 1 minute. Sprinkle cream cheese on top of eggs. Bake for 3 to 5 minutes or until eggs are set. Remove from oven and sprinkle with freshly ground pepper. Cut into 6 wedges. Serve immediately.

MAKES 1 10-INCH (25-CM) OMELET.

Hunk's Straw Potatoes

HUNK: Well, your head ain't made of straw, you know!

2 medium potatoes, peeled and grated (about 2 cups)
2 tablespoons flour
2 tablespoons (28 g) unsalted butter, melted
¼ teaspoon salt
⅛ teaspoon freshly ground black pepper

vegetable oil for frying
4 ounces (114 g) sour cream
4 ounces (114 g) smoked salmon, thinly sliced

In a medium bowl, mix together grated potatoes, flour, melted butter, salt, and pepper. Heat a skillet with just enough vegetable oil to coat bottom. Drop potato mixture by teaspoonful into hot pan to make small potato pancakes. Cook over medium-high heat, turning once to brown both sides. Remove cooked pancakes and drain on paper towels. Serve while warm with a small dollop of sour cream and a piece of smoked salmon on each pancake.

MAKES ABOUT 2 DOZEN 3-INCH (8-CM) PANCAKES.

KANSAS CORNMEAL PANCAKES

2 tablespoons sugar
1 cup (140 g) all-purpose flour
1 cup (145 g) yellow cornmeal
½ teaspoon salt
1½ teaspoons baking powder
2 large eggs
1½ cups (360 ml) whole milk or 1¼ cups (300 ml) low-fat milk
6 tablespoons (85 g) unsalted butter, melted

In a medium mixing bowl, stir dry ingredients together. Make a small well in center. Put eggs in well and begin to whisk at center, working slowly toward the sides. While whisking, pour the milk into the center in a thin, even stream. Mix until all the milk and dry ingredients are incorporated. Whisk in melted butter. Make pancakes in a nonstick skillet or in a skillet brushed with oil. Serve with Bluebird's Blueberry Syrup.

MAKES ABOUT 2 DOZEN 1½-INCH (8-CM) PANCAKES.

BLUEBIRD'S BLUEBERRY SYRUP

¾ cup (100 g) frozen blueberries, thawed and drained
¾ cup (180 ml) pure maple syrup

Cook blueberries and syrup in a small saucepan over low heat for about 10 minutes, until mixture is thick and simmering. Serve hot with Kansas Cornmeal Pancakes.

MAKES ABOUT 1½ CUPS (360 ML) SYRUP.

★ CASTING QUIZ ★

Whom did MGM producers originally want to play Dorothy, the Scarecrow, the Tin Man, the Wizard, and the Witch?
Dorothy—Shirley Temple; the Scarecrow—Buddy Ebsen; the Tin Man—Ray Bolger; the Wizard—W. C. Fields; and the Witch—Gale Sondergaard.

MISS GULCH'S SOUR CHERRY KUCHEN

MISS GULCH: *(sharply) I want to see you and your wife right away about Dorothy.*
UNCLE HENRY: *(worried) Dorothy? Well, what has Dorothy done?*
MISS GULCH: *(indignantly) What's she done? I'm all but lame from the bite on my leg!*
UNCLE HENRY: *You mean she bit ya?*
MISS GULCH: *No, her dog!*
UNCLE HENRY: *Oh, she bit her dog, eh?*

2 cups (280 g) all-purpose flour
1½ teaspoons baking soda
½ cup (100 g) sugar
pinch salt
2 large eggs
¼ cup (57 g) unsalted butter, melted
⅓ cup (80 g) sour cream
1 teaspoon vanilla extract
½ teaspoon almond extract
1½ cups (360 ml) milk

FILLING AND TOPPING
¼ cup (35 g) all-purpose flour
½ cup (120 g) firmly packed brown sugar
½ cup (50 g) rolled oats
½ cup (50 g) sliced almonds
2 tablespoons (28 g) unsalted butter, melted
2 cups (400 g) fresh or canned sour cherries, pitted and drained

Butter and flour a 9-inch (23-cm) springform pan. Set aside. Preheat oven to 350°F (180°C). Sift dry ingredients for cake into a medium bowl. Whisk together eggs, butter, sour cream, extracts, and milk. Make a well in the center of the dry ingredients. Pour egg mixture into well and stir slowly with whisk until completely blended.

For filling and topping, stir together flour, butter, brown sugar, oats, and almonds in a medium bowl. Spoon ½ of batter into pan and spread to edges. Cover with cherries and ½ of filling. Spoon remaining batter on top and then cover with remaining filling. Bake for 55 to 60 minutes, until toothpick inserted into center comes out clean. Let cool 5 minutes in pan on cake rack. Unmold from springform pan. Serve warm or at room temperature.

MAKES 10 SERVINGS.

AUNTIE EM'S CRULLERS

AUNT EM: *Here—here—can't work on an empty stomach.*
   Have some crullers.
HUNK: *Gosh, Mrs. Gale!*
HICKORY: *Oh, thanks.*
AUNT EM: *Just fried.*

1 envelope or ¼ ounce (7 g) dry yeast
3 tablespoons warm water
1 tablespoon granulated sugar
¾ cup (180 ml) whole milk
¼ cup (52 g) sour cream
¼ cup (75 g) honey
¼ cup (60 g) firmly packed brown sugar
2 large eggs
3½ cups (490 g) all-purpose flour (for nuttier-flavored crullers, substitute
¼ cup whole-wheat flour for ¼ cup of all-purpose flour)
2 teaspoons ground cinnamon
1 teaspoon ground ginger
1 teaspoon salt
2 quarts (2 liters) vegetable oil for frying
honey or confectioners' sugar

In a large mixing bowl, dissolve yeast in warm water. Add granulated sugar and let stand until yeast bubbles, about 5 minutes. Meanwhile gently heat milk, sour cream, honey, and brown sugar, but do not boil. Stir eggs into yeast mixture, and then stir in warm milk mixture. Add remaining ingredients and beat with an electric mixer for 3 minutes. Scrape sides of bowl. Cover with plastic wrap and let rise in a warm place until doubled in volume, about 1½ hours. Heat oil to 350°F (180°C) in a large, heavy-bottomed pot. On a floured surface, roll golf-ball-size pieces of dough into 5-inch (13-cm) lengths using floured

hands (dough is sticky). Then twist and pinch edges to seal. Lower crullers one at a time into hot oil and fry about 3 to 4 minutes, turning once, until golden brown. Drain on paper towels and serve with warm honey or sprinkle with powdered sugar.

MAKES 1½ DOZEN CRULLERS.

OVER THE RAINBOW FRUIT PLATES

Somewhere, over the rainbow, skies are blue,
And the dreams that you dare to dream really do come true.

1 kiwi
1 small bunch seedless black grapes
5 strawberries
1 orange
1 ruby grapefruit
½ cantaloupe
1 banana

YOGURT SAUCE
8 ounces (227 g) plain low-fat yogurt
1½ tablespoons brown sugar

Peel and slice kiwi into thin slices. Cut grapes in half. Hull and thinly slice strawberries lengthwise. Cut orange and grapefruit into segments. Peel and thinly slice cantaloupe and banana. Arrange fruit in a rainbow-like arc on each of 4 individual plates. Layer the different kinds of fruit in rows of different colors.

For yogurt sauce, whisk ingredients together in a small bowl until smooth and serve on the side.

MAKES 4 SERVINGS.

LEMON DROP MUFFINS

Someday I'll wish upon a star
And wake up where the clouds are far behind me,
Where troubles melt like lemon drops . . .

¼ cup (57 g) unsalted butter, at room temperature
1 cup (200 g) sugar
2 large eggs
2 tablespoons lemon juice
1 tablespoon grated lemon zest
1 vanilla bean, split and seeds scraped out
2 cups (280 g) all-purpose flour
1½ teaspoons baking powder
¼ teaspoon salt
¾ cup (180 ml) milk

Preheat oven to 375°F (190°C). Grease 12 muffin cups or line with paper. Beat butter and sugar in a mixing bowl until light and fluffy. Add eggs, one at a time, beating after each addition. Add lemon juice, zest, and vanilla bean seeds. In a small bowl, stir together flour, baking powder, and salt. Stir milk and dry ingredients alternately into butter mixture until they are incorporated into a smooth batter. Spoon into muffin pans. Bake for 20 to 25 minutes.

MAKES 12 MUFFINS.

★ LEMON TWISTER ★

What special effect in The Wizard of Oz did not work initially?
Creating the tornado was the most costly and difficult special effect. Actually a miniature, the first cyclone failed because it didn't twist, a mistake that cost MGM $8,000. (From Aljean Harmetz, The Making of the Wizard of Oz, *Delta, 1977.)*

ORANGE TWISTER

ZEKE: It's a twister . . . it's a twister!

1½ ounces (45 ml) gin
4 ounces (120 ml) orange juice
4 ounces (120 ml) ginger ale
orange peel

Pour gin and orange juice into a tall glass filled with ice. Stir and add ginger ale. Garnish with a long twist of orange peel. Serve immediately.

MAKES 1 DRINK.

PROFESSOR MARVEL'S FROZEN KANSAS KAPPUCCINO

1½ cups (360 ml) strong brewed coffee
6 ounces (180 ml) milk
4 ounces (120 ml) chocolate liqueur
2 ounces (60 ml) heavy cream
ground cinnamon or chocolate shavings

Freeze coffee in an ice cube tray the day before making this drink. In a blender, mix coffee ice cubes, milk, and chocolate liqueur until ice is crushed. Add heavy cream and continue to blend until light and frothy, about 30 seconds more. If too thick, add milk to thin. Serve in chilled tall glasses. Sprinkle with cinnamon or garnish with chocolate shavings.

MAKES 4 DRINKS.

KIDS PARTY ★ IN ♥ MUNCHKINLAND

MUNCHKIN NO. 1:

We thank you very sweetly
For doing it so neatly.

Glinda's Magic Wand Star Cookies

GLINDA: Come out, come out, wherever you are.
And meet the young lady who fell from a star.

2½ cups (350 g) all-purpose flour
½ teaspoon salt
1 teaspoon ground cinnamon
¾ cup (170 g) unsalted butter, at room temperature
½ cup (120 g) firmly packed light brown sugar
½ cup (100 g) granulated sugar
1 large egg
½ cup (105 g) sour cream
1 teaspoon vanilla extract

In a small mixing bowl, stir together flour, salt, and cinnamon. Set aside. In a food processor or mixing bowl, beat butter and sugars together until light and fluffy. Add egg and continue beating until incorporated. Beat in sour cream and vanilla. Fold in dry ingredients. Chill dough until firm, about 1 hour. Roll out dough to ¼ inch (6 mm) thick. Cut out cookies with star cutter or template. To use template on opposite page, first trace star onto a piece of cardboard. Cut out the star shape from cardboard, place on the rolled dough, and cut stars out of dough with a knife. Reroll dough scraps and repeat. Place on ungreased cookie sheets and place in freezer. When ready to assemble, preheat oven to 350°F (180°C). Remove stars from the freezer, and place one star cookie on an empty ungreased baking sheet. Put popsicle stick on cookie and press gently. Place a second star on top. Repeat with remaining stars. Sprinkle with decorative sugar. Bake 10 to 12 minutes at 350°F (180°C) until lightly golden. Let sit for 3 minutes, and then remove with spatula from baking sheet and let cool on wire rack.

MAKES 2 DOZEN COOKIES.

Star
template

Munchkinland Pink Party Cake

DOROTHY: *Toto, I've a feeling we're not in Kansas anymore . . .*
We must be over the rainbow!
Suddenly a large, pink-tinted crystal BUBBLE, gleaming like a
soap bubble, approaches getting bigger and bigger.

2 cups (280 g) cake flour

2 teaspoons baking powder

¼ teaspoon salt

6 large eggs, separated

1½ cups (300 g) sugar

½ cup (120 ml) vegetable oil

½ cup (120 ml) milk

1 tablespoon vanilla extract

FILLING AND ICING

1 pint (454 g) raspberries
12 ounces (340 g) fresh or frozen pitted peaches, peeled and chopped
1 cup (200 g) sugar
3 cups (720 ml) heavy cream
1 teaspoon vanilla extract
red food coloring

Preheat oven to 350°F (180°C). Grease and flour a 10-inch (25-cm) round cake pan. In a small bowl, stir together flour, baking powder, and salt. Set aside. In a large bowl, with a whisk or beater, beat egg yolks with sugar until light. Stir in oil, milk, and vanilla until well blended. Fold in dry ingredients until there are no lumps. In a clean bowl, beat egg whites until soft peaks form. Fold into cake batter. Pour batter into prepared pan and bake about 45 minutes, until cake is set in center. Unmold cake from pan and let cool completely.

While cake is cooling, make filling and icing. Stir together ¾ of the raspberries and all the peaches with ½ cup (100 g) sugar in a medium bowl. Set aside. Whip cream with ½ cup (100 g) sugar, vanilla, and a few drops of red food coloring until the icing is a pale pink color.

Slice cake into 4 layers. Place first layer on a cake plate. Top with ⅓ of fruit mixture and a ½-inch (13-mm) layer of whipped cream. Repeat with other layers, ending with fourth layer of cake. Ice cake with remaining whipped cream and garnish with reserved raspberries. Cake is best when eaten the same day that it is assembled. (Cake can be baked a day or two ahead, wrapped in plastic, and assembled on day of party).

MAKES 1 10-INCH (25-CM) CAKE.

Wicked Witch Waffles

ALL OF THE MUNCHKINS: *The house began to pitch.*
The kitchen took a slitch.
It landed on the Wicked Witch in the middle of a ditch
Which
Was not a healthy sitch-
Uation for The Wicked Witch

2 cups (280 g) all-purpose flour
½ teaspoon salt
1 teaspoon baking soda
2 teaspoons baking powder
4 large eggs
½ cup (150 g) honey
⅔ cup (140 g) plain yogurt
1⅓ cups (320 ml) milk
2 teaspoons vanilla extract
½ cup (114 g) unsalted butter, melted
½ gallon (1.8 kg) vanilla frozen yogurt
2 pints (454 g) fresh strawberries, hulled, sliced, and tossed with
1 tablespoon sugar

In a medium bowl, mix flour, salt, baking soda, and baking powder. Set aside. In a separate bowl, whisk together eggs, honey, and yogurt. Whisk milk slowly into egg mixture, and then add vanilla extract. Make a well in center of dry ingredients. Pour milk mixture slowly into center while whisking continuously. Beat until smooth. Whisk in butter. Cook waffles in waffle iron according to manufacturer's instructions. Serve waffles warm with a scoop of yogurt and a spoonful of sliced strawberries.

MAKES ABOUT 15 WAFFLES.

Yellow Brickle Road Brownies

DOROTHY: *But how do I start for Emerald City?*
GLINDA: *It's always best to start at the beginning. And all you do is follow the Yellow Brick Road.*

6 ounces (170 g) unsweetened chocolate

¾ cup (170 g) unsalted butter

3 large eggs

2¼ cups (450 g) sugar

1 tablespoon vanilla extract

1½ cups (210 g) all-purpose flour

¾ cup (73 g) chopped walnuts (optional)

ICING

8 ounces (227 g) cream cheese, at room temperature

1 cup (120 g) confectioners' sugar

few drops food coloring

6 ounces (170 g) brickle bits or crushed brickle bars

Preheat oven to 350°F (180°C). Grease and flour an 11 x 7-inch (28 x 18-cm) pan. Melt butter and chocolate in a small bowl over a pot of gently simmering water (or in microwave on medium for about 3 minutes). Meanwhile, whisk eggs, sugar, and vanilla until smooth and fluffy. Stir in melted butter and chocolate until blended. Fold in flour and walnuts. Pour into prepared pan. Bake for 35 to 40 minutes or until cake tester comes out clean. Let cool completely.

When brownies are cool, prepare the icing. Beat cream cheese, confectioners' sugar, and food coloring until blended. Spread evenly over top of brownies. Sprinkle brickle over top of brownies. Chill for at least an hour before cutting into squares. Store in refrigerator.

MAKES 15 2-INCH (5-CM) BROWNIES.

Munchkin Mayor's Chocolate Peanut Butter Pie

MAYOR: (singing)
> As Mayor of the Munchkin City
> In the County of the Land of Oz,
> I welcome you most regally.

1 recipe chocolate wafer crust (see p. 63)
3 2-ounce (28-g) candy bars
(those with chocolate and peanuts work well)
½ cup (100 g) sugar
12 ounces (340 g) cream cheese, softened
2 large eggs
⅓ cup (80 g) sour cream
½ cup (140 g) peanut butter

Preheat oven to 450°F (230°C). Press chocolate wafer crust onto bottom and sides of a 9-inch (23-cm) pie pan. Bake pie crust for 5 minutes. Remove from oven and let cool. Reduce oven temperature to 325°F (165°C). Cut candy bars in half lengthwise and then cut into ¼-inch (6-mm) pieces. Scatter candy bar pieces over bottom of baked crust. In a small bowl, combine the sugar and cream cheese. Beat until smooth. Add eggs, one at a time, beating well after each. Add sour cream and peanut butter and beat until smooth. Pour over candy bar pieces. Bake for 30 to 40 minutes or until center is set. Cool completely. Refrigerate for 2 to 3 hours before serving. Store in refrigerator.

MAKES 8 TO 10 SERVINGS.

Lullaby League Banana Fudge Sundaes

TINY TOTS: (singing as they dance on toe)
We represent the Lullaby League, the Lullaby League, the
Lullaby League,
And in the name of the Lullaby League
We wish to welcome you to Munchkinland.

2 cups (280 g) all-purpose flour
½ teaspoon salt
1½ teaspoons baking soda
¾ cup (170 g) butter, at room temperature
1½ cups (200 g) sugar
3 large eggs
3 ripe bananas, peeled and mashed
½ gallon (1.8 kg) vanilla ice cream
1 recipe Tiny Tots Chocolate Sauce

Preheat oven to 350°F (180°C). Butter and flour a 6-cup (1.5-liter) loaf pan. Sift flour, salt, and baking soda together in a small bowl. Set aside. Cream butter and sugar together in a medium bowl until light and fluffy. Add eggs one at a time. Add mashed bananas and beat until incorporated. Fold in dry ingredients. Pour into prepared pan. Bake for about 1 hour, until cake tester comes out clean. The cake will be very dark in color. Let cool for 5 minutes. Unmold from pan and let cool completely. Store at room temperature.

When ready to serve sundaes, slice loaf into 12 slices. Place each slice in an ice cream dish. Top with a scoop of vanilla ice cream and warm chocolate sauce.

MAKES 12 SUNDAES.

Tiny Tots Chocolate Sauce

1 pound (454 g) semisweet chocolate chips
2 cups (480 ml) whole milk

Place chocolate chips in a medium bowl. Bring milk to a boil in a small saucepan. Pour hot milk over chocolate chips. Whisk until completely blended. Serve warm.

MAKES 3 CUPS.

Five Little Fiddlers Fruit Shake

FIVE LITTLE FIDDLERS *dance out behind* **DOROTHY** *and lead the procession of* **MUNCHKINS** *behind her and* **TOTO.**

You're off to see the Wizard,
The Wonderful Wizard of Oz.
You'll find he is a Whiz of a Wiz
if ever a Wiz there was.

2 ripe bananas, peeled
1 cup (240 ml) orange juice
3 tablespoons honey
1 tablespoon lime juice
1 cup (120 g) crushed ice
banana slices
grated lime zest

Whirl all ingredients in a blender or food processor until smooth and fluffy. Pour into a tall glass with crushed ice. Garnish with banana slices and lime zest.

MAKES 2 SHAKES.

For how much did Christie's East auction one pair of Dorothy's ruby slippers in 1988?

$165,000, the highest price paid to that time for a piece of movie memorabilia, and the highest price ever paid at auction for an article of costume.

Ruby Slipper Cookies

WITCH: *They're gone! The ruby slippers—what have you done with them? Give them to me or I'll—*
GLINDA: *It's too late!*
(She points her wand at DOROTHY's feet.)
There they are, and there they'll stay!

1 cup (227 g) unsalted butter, at room temperature
1 cup (200 g) sugar
1 large egg
1 teaspoon vanilla extract
grated zest of 1 lemon
¼ teaspoon salt
2½ cups (350 g) all-purpose flour
red crystal sugar for decoration

Beat butter and sugar until light and fluffy. Add egg, vanilla, lemon zest, and salt. Continue to beat until well blended. Fold flour into dough until incorporated. Wrap dough and chill several hours or overnight. Preheat oven to 350°F (180°C). On a lightly floured surface, roll dough ¼ inch (6 mm) thick. Using the template pictured opposite and a small sharp knife, cut out slipper shapes. To use template, see directions for star cookies (p. 18). Place cookies on a cookie sheet lined with waxed paper or parchment. Sprinkle red crystal sugar on slippers and press lightly. Bake about 10 minutes. Cool on racks.

MAKES 2½ DOZEN COOKIES.

Ruby Slipper template

★ MUNCHKIN TALLY ★

How many munchkins were there?

MGM employed 124 little people for The Wizard of Oz, the most midgets
and dwarves ever to work on a film.

★ MUNCHKIN TOPPINGS ★

From head to toe, each munchkin costume was specially designed by Adrian
and adorned with the likes of buckles, buttons, bows, tassels, pompoms,
flowers, flowerpots, birds, and bird cages. Provide kids with an assortment
of fanciful materials and have them create their own munchkin hats.

Munchkin Muffin Sandwiches

MINI CARROT MUFFINS
2 large eggs
¾ cup (180 ml) milk
⅔ cup (160 ml) corn oil
½ cup (120 g) firmly packed brown sugar
2 cups (200 g) shredded carrots
½ cup (70 g) golden raisins
2½ cups (350 g) all-purpose flour
1 tablespoon baking powder
1 teaspoon salt
1 teaspoon ground cinnamon
½ teaspoon ground ginger

FILLING
1 pound (454 g) cream cheese
8¼ ounces (234 g) crushed pineapple
3 tablespoons honey
1½ teaspoons ground cinnamon

Preheat oven to 400°F (200°C). In a small bowl, combine eggs, milk, oil, brown sugar, carrots, and raisins. In a larger bowl, combine flour, baking powder, salt, and spices. Stir egg mixture into dry ingredients until thoroughly combined. Grease miniature muffin tins and fill with batter. Bake for 15 minutes or until lightly browned. Cool and unmold.

To make filling, beat cream cheese with an electric mixer or spoon until smooth. Stir in three remaining ingredients. To make muffin sandwiches, cut muffins in half lengthwise and fill with a heaping teaspoonful of cream cheese filling. Replace muffin tops.

MAKES ABOUT 2½ DOZEN MUFFIN SANDWICHES.

Da Lollipop Guild Lollipops

8 ounces (227 g) white chocolate, coarsely chopped
8 ounces (227 g) semisweet or milk chocolate, coarsely chopped
½ teaspoon vegetable oil
¾ cup (150 g) chocolate-covered raisins or other small chocolate candies
10 lollipop sticks or drink stirrers

Line 2 baking sheets with foil. Cut 10 pieces of foil into 12 x 4-inch (30 x 10-cm) strips. Fold these 10 pieces into 12 x 1-inch (30 x 2-cm) strips. Shape strips into circles with a 3-inch (8-cm) circumference. Tape to close. Place foil circles on baking sheets and place sheets in freezer. In a small bowl over barely simmering water, melt white chocolate. Stir until smooth. Set aside. In another small bowl over barely simmering water, melt semisweet chocolate. Whisk in oil and stir until smooth. Spoon 2 rounded teaspoonfuls of white chocolate and two rounded teaspoonfuls of semisweet chocolate into each foil circle. Sprinkle with chocolate candy. Let lollipops set for about 5 to 10 minutes until chocolate is still soft but not runny. Carefully remove foil circles from chocolate. Press lollipop sticks into center of lollipops. Let set completely. Store lollipops on baking sheet in a cool dry place or in refrigerator until ready to use.

MAKES 10 3-INCH (8-CM) LOLLIPOPS.

APPETIZERS ON THE YELLOW BRICK ROAD

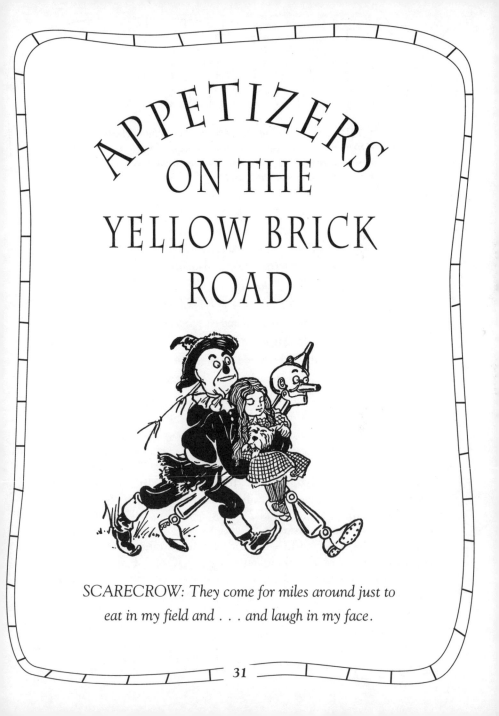

SCARECROW: *They come for miles around just to eat in my field and . . . and laugh in my face.*

SAUSAGE-STUFFED BROOMSTICK

DOROTHY: *The Wizard of Oz? Is he good or is he wicked?*
GLINDA: *Oh, very good; but very mysterious. He lives in the Emerald City, and that's a long journey from here. Did you bring your broomstick with you?*

1 long loaf French or Italian bread
4 tablespoons (60 ml) olive oil
12 ounces (340 g) Italian sausage, casings removed
½ cup (60 g) chopped onion
1 large clove garlic, minced
2½ cups (200 g) coarsely chopped eggplant
1 cup (50 g) washed and chopped spinach
1 teaspoon dried oregano
salt and freshly ground black pepper to taste
2 tablespoons grated Parmesan cheese
2 tablespoons raisins

Cut bread in half crosswise. Using a fork, remove center of bread from both halves, leaving ¼ inch (6 mm) of bread in the crust. Discard crumbs. In a medium skillet, heat 1 tablespoon oil. Fry sausage in oil over medium heat until cooked through, crumbling sausage as it browns. Remove sausage from skillet and drain on paper towels. Pour excess grease from skillet. Add 2 tablespoons oil to skillet and heat over low flame until oil is warm. Add onion and garlic. Sauté over low heat until onion is translucent. Add remaining tablespoon oil. Add eggplant and continue cooking until eggplant is soft, about 5 minutes. Add spinach and oregano. Season to taste with salt and pepper. Cook for 1 minute. Remove pan from heat. Add cooked sausage, cheese, and raisins to pan.

Fill cavity of each half loaf with sausage-eggplant mixture, packing tightly with back of a spoon. Wrap each bread half with aluminum foil or plastic wrap. Refrigerate at least 3 hours or overnight. Before serving, preheat oven to 325°F (165°C). Unwrap bread and heat on a baking sheet for 10 to 15 minutes, until heated through. Remove from oven and slice into ⅓-inch (8-mm) slices with a sharp knife.

MAKES 15 TO 20 SLICES.

CORNFIELD CRUNCH

SCARECROW: *I could while away the hours*
Conferrin' with the flowers
Consultin' with the rain
And my head, I'd be scratchin'
While my thoughts were busy hatchin'
If I only had a brain.

2 cups (50 g) corn flakes
2 cups (25 g) popped popcorn
2 cups (40 g) corn puffs
2 cups (50 g) corn chex
2 cups (260 g) lightly salted peanuts
6 tablespoons (85 g) unsalted butter, melted
½ teaspoon paprika
½ teaspoon salt
¼ teaspoon cayenne pepper (optional)

Preheat oven to 350°F (180°C). In a large bowl, mix corn flakes, popcorn, corn puffs, chex, and peanuts. In a small saucepan, stir together melted butter, paprika, salt, and cayenne. Pour evenly over cereal mixture. Toss to coat cereal with butter. Spread mixture on 2 cookie sheets. Bake for 15 minutes. Cool on cookie sheets.

MAKES 8 CUPS (510 G).

TALKING TREES' APPLE BISCUITS

FIRST TREE: *Well, how would you like to have someone come along and pick something off of you?*
DOROTHY: *Oh, dear! I keep forgetting I'm not in Kansas.*
SCARECROW: *Come along, Dorothy, you don't want any of those apples. Hmmm!*
FIRST TREE: *Are you hinting my apples aren't what they ought to be?*
SCARECROW: *Oh, no! It's just that she doesn't like little green worms!*

2 cups (280 g) all-purpose flour
pinch salt
1½ teaspoons baking soda
2 tablespoons baking powder
6 tablespoons (85 g) cold unsalted butter, cut into small pieces
¾ cup (158 g) plain yogurt
1 large egg yolk
2 tablespoons apple juice or cider
1 cup (120 g) coarsely chopped unpeeled red apples

Place flour, salt, baking soda, and baking powder in a mixing bowl. Cut in butter with fingers or pastry blender until mixture resembles coarse meal. Mix yogurt, egg yolk, juice, and apples in a small bowl. Stir yogurt mixture into flour with wooden spoon until a dough is formed. Roll dough out on lightly floured surface ¾ inch (18 mm) thick. Cut biscuits with 2-inch (5-cm) round cutter. Place on a baking sheet lined with waxed paper or parchment. Bake at 375°F (190°C) for 12 to 13 minutes, until lightly browned. To serve as an hors d'oeuvre, slice biscuits in half and spread bottom half with honey mustard. Top with a slice of apple and a slice of smoked turkey or ham. Replace top.

MAKES 1½ DOZEN BISCUITS.

★ SCATTERBRAINED CRANE ★

For the apple orchard sequence, 300 birds were rented from the Zoo Park in Los Angeles so that the director could choose a few for the background. A Saurus crane went after Ray Bolger's straw stuffing, sending him to his dressing room until the bird could be restrained. (From Aljean Harmetz, The Making of The Wizard of Oz, Delta, 1977.)

SUN-DRIED TOMATO HEARTS

TIN MAN: **When a man's an empty kettle**
He should be on his mettle
And yet I'm torn apart
Just because I'm presumin'
That I could be kind-a human
If I only had a heart.

1 loaf white sandwich bread
6 ounces (150 g) sun-dried tomatoes packed in oil, drained, oil reserved
2 cloves garlic
5 tablespoons oil from jar of tomatoes
2 tablespoons ground walnuts
3 tablespoons (15 g) chopped parsley
¼ teaspoon salt
2 ounces (60 g) grated Parmesan cheese

With a heart-shaped cookie cutter, cut out hearts from each slice of bread, discarding crusts. Toast hearts on a baking sheet in a 375°F (190°C) oven until very light brown, about 5 minutes. Purée tomatoes with garlic cloves in a food processor or blender. Add oil, walnuts, parsley, and salt and process until homogenous. Stir in cheese. Spread mixture onto heart-shaped toasts and serve.

MAKES ABOUT 20 TOASTS.

FIERY FILET

WITCH: And you! I'll use you for a beehive! Here, Scarecrow!
Want to play ball?
SCARECROW: Oh! Look out! Fire! I'm burning! I'm burning!
Oh! Take it away!

2 pounds (908 g) trimmed beef tenderloin, 8 x 2½ inches (20 x 6 cm)
¼ cup (60 ml) olive oil
2 cloves garlic, minced
1 teaspoon salt
1 teaspoon freshly ground black pepper
½ teaspoon cayenne pepper
1 tablespoon dried oregano
2 teaspoons dried thyme
1 teaspoon paprika
¼ cup (60 ml) vegetable oil
1 loaf French or Italian bread
¼ cup (55 g) prepared mayonnaise
1 tablespoon chopped fresh dill
1 tablespoon chopped fresh parsley
sprigs fresh dill or parsley (optional)

Rub tenderloin with olive oil and minced garlic. Wrap and let sit 1 hour at room temperature or in refrigerator overnight. In a small bowl, stir together salt, black pepper, cayenne, oregano, thyme, and paprika. Coat filet with spice mixture. Preheat oven to 400°F (200°C). Heat a 10- or 12-inch (25- or 30-cm) cast-iron skillet until smoking (about 5 minutes on high heat). Place filet in pan and pour vegetable oil over it. (Be careful because oil may flame if pan is too hot). Reduce heat to medium. Cook meat until spices on outside are blackened on all sides, about 7 minutes. Bake filet in oven for 10 to 15 minutes, until it is cooked to taste. Remove from oven. Chill filet until ready to serve.

Contents

Slice bread into ½-inch (13-mm) slices. Toast in oven and set aside until ready to use. Mix mayonnaise with chopped herbs and chill until ready to use. To serve, slice cold filet into ¼-inch (6-mm) slices. Spread toasts with herb mayonnaise and top with slice of filet and sprig of parsley or dill if desired.

MAKES 24 HORS D'OEUVRES.

PARMESAN POPPY WAFERS

WITCH: *Poppies . . . poppies . . . poppies will put them to sleep . . . sleep . . . now they'll sleep . . .*

8 ounces (227 g) puff pastry dough
¾ cup (90 g) grated Parmesan cheese
¼ cup (35 g) poppy seeds

Preheat oven to 400°F (200°C). Roll half of puff pastry dough on a lightly floured surface to ⅛ inch (3 mm) thick. Sprinkle evenly with ½ of the Parmesan cheese and ½ of the poppy seeds. Continue to roll pastry dough carefully, pressing cheese and seeds into dough, until it is ¹⁄₁₆ inch (1.5 mm) thick. Cut dough into 2-inch (5-cm) squares with a sharp knife. Repeat with remaining half of puff pastry. Place squares on ungreased baking sheets. Freeze for 10 minutes or longer. If making for a later time, you may at this point wrap and freeze the dough for up to 1 month. Remove from freezer and bake at 400°F (200°C) for 10 to 12 minutes or until lightly browned. Do not overbake.

MAKES 30 WAFERS.

SPELLBOUND SNOW CRAB MUSHROOMS

SCARECROW: (trying to lift DOROTHY) Uh! Oh, this is terrible! Can't budge her an inch! This is a spell, this is!

TIN MAN: It's the Wicked Witch! What'll we do? HELP! HELP!

SCARECROW: It's no use screaming at a time like this! Nobody will hear you! . . . HELP! HELP! HELP! (now looking up in wonder) It's snowing!

LION: Ah—ah. Unusual weather we're havin', ain't we?

2 tablespoons olive oil

½ cup (100 g) red bell pepper, finely chopped

½ medium yellow onion, finely chopped

1 clove garlic, minced

6 ounces (170 g) crabmeat, cleaned (fresh, frozen, or canned)

1 teaspoon dry mustard

2 teaspoons Old Bay Seasoning (or other shellfish seasoning)

2 tablespoons mayonnaise

juice of ½ lemon

dash Worcestershire sauce

3 tablespoons minced fresh parsley

12 ounces (340 g) mushrooms (about 15 medium to large), stemmed and cleaned

Preheat oven to 400°F (200°C). Heat 1 tablespoon olive oil in a medium skillet. Add the red pepper, onion, and garlic and sauté over medium heat until onion is translucent, about 2 minutes. Set aside to cool. In a medium bowl, combine crabmeat, dry mustard, Old Bay Seasoning, mayonnaise, lemon juice, Worcestershire sauce, and parsley. Add onion mixture. Toss mushroom caps with remaining tablespoon of olive oil. Stuff each cap with crab mixture, mounding it slightly. Place mushrooms on a baking sheet and bake for 25 to 30 minutes or until lightly browned on top. Serve hot. This recipe can be prepared up to 8 hours ahead and refrigerated until ready to bake.

MAKES 15 MUSHROOMS.

PUT 'EM UP PECAN PUFFS

LION: (growling) Hah, put 'em up, put 'em up! Which one of ya first? I'll fight ya both together if ya want. . . . Oh, scared, huh? Afraid, huh? Ha! How long can ya stay fresh in that can? (laughs) Come on! Get up and fight, ya shiverin' junkyard.

1½ cups (360 ml) water
6 tablespoons (85 g) unsalted butter, cut into pieces
½ teaspoon salt
1 cup (140 g) sifted all-purpose flour
3 large eggs
1 teaspoon dry mustard
¼ teaspoon paprika
¾ cup (50 g) shredded Cheddar cheese
¾ cup (75 g) chopped pecans

Preheat oven to 350°F (180°C). Line 2 baking sheets with waxed paper or parchment, then grease the paper. In a small saucepan, bring water to a boil with butter and salt. When butter is completely melted, reduce heat to medium, add flour, and stir rapidly with a wooden spoon until a sticky dough is formed. Continue stirring over medium heat for another minute. Transfer dough to a medium bowl. With an electric mixer, beat in eggs, one at a time. Then beat in mustard and paprika until incorporated. Stir in cheese and pecans by hand. Drop dough by well-rounded tablespoons onto prepared baking sheets. Bake 35 to 40 minutes or until nicely browned. Serve warm.

MAKES ABOUT 30 PUFFS.

COWARDLY CRUDITES WITH GOAT CHEESE DIP

LION: *All right, I'll go in there for Dorothy—Wicked Witch or no Wicked Witch—guards or no guards—I'll tear 'em apart—Woof! I may not come out alive, but I'm goin' in there! There's only one thing I want you fellas to do.*
SCARECROW and TIN MAN: *What's that?*
LION: *Talk me out of it!*

8 ounces (227 g) fresh goat cheese, at room temperature
1½ cups (340 g) sour cream
4 scallions, finely chopped
⅓ cup (20 g) minced fresh dill
⅓ cup (20 g) minced fresh mint
2 tablespoons minced fresh parsley
½ teaspoon salt
freshly ground black pepper to taste
juice of ½ lemon
assortment of raw vegetables, cut up

In a medium bowl, mash goat cheese with the back of a spoon. Stir in sour cream and blend until smooth. Add remaining ingredients except vegetables and combine thoroughly. Arrange a colorful selection of cut-up vegetables in a large basket or on a platter. Serve with dip.

MAKES ABOUT 2½ CUPS (625 G) DIP.

Where did Ray Bolger, Jack Haley, and Bert Lahr eat during filming?
They ate together in a bungalow on the MGM lot. When they tried once to dine in the commissary, they were turned away because their faces covered with rubber and fur and aluminum paste offended the other diners.

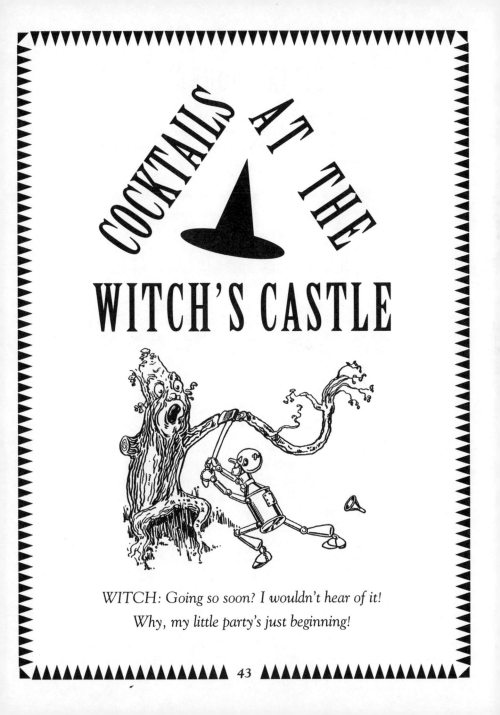

COCKTAILS AT THE
WITCH'S CASTLE

WITCH: Going so soon? I wouldn't hear of it!
Why, my little party's just beginning!

FLYING MONKEY

WITCH: *(addressing the WINGED MONKEYS) Take your army to the Haunted Forest and bring me that girl and her dog. Do what you like with the others, but I want her alive and unharmed!*

1 ounce (30 ml) dark rum
1 ounce (30 ml) creme de banana
1 tablespoon lime juice
1 ripe banana, peeled
1 tablespoon sugar (preferably superfine)
1 cup (120 g) crushed ice

In a food processor or blender, whirl all ingredients except crushed ice for one minute, until light and creamy. Add crushed ice and blend for 30 seconds. Pour into a tall chilled glass.

MAKES 1 DRINK.

★ MONKEY BUSINESS ★

A group of small, thin men were hired for $20 to dangle from wire as Winged Monkeys and swoop down upon Dorothy, the Tin Man, the Scarecrow, and the Cowardly Lion. A dispute erupted when the men thought they were getting $20 for each time they were hoisted up and flown again, but the studio claimed they were actors hired for $20 a day. Jack Haley recalled: "Some guy came from the Screen Actors Guild and it was the most ludicrous thing you've ever seen in your life. All those monkeys standing on chairs and shouting at him. I think the studio made some sort of settlement, gave them a little added money." (From Aljean Harmetz,
The Making of the Wizard of Oz, Delta, 1977.)

HAUNTED FOREST BUTTERNUT MILKSHAKE

LION: *Do—do ya think it'll be polite, droppin' in like this?*

1 pint (227 g) butter pecan ice cream
½ cup (120 ml) milk
1 cup (120 g) crushed ice
3 ounces (90 ml) hazelnut liqueur

In a food processor or blender, whirl all ingredients until creamy and well blended. If shake is too thick, use more milk to thin. Serve in tall chilled glasses.

MAKES 2 SHAKES.

RUSTY TIN MAN

TIN MAN: *I'm afraid I'm a little rusty yet.*

1½ ounces (45 ml) scotch
1 ounce (30 ml) Campari
4 ounces (120 ml) seltzer
lemon peel twist

In a tall glass filled with ice, pour scotch, Campari, and seltzer. Stir. Garnish with lemon twist and serve immediately.

MAKES 1 DRINK.

WHITE WINE WELCOME SANGRIA

WITCH: *(with diabolical sweetness) What a nice little dog. (puts him in the basket and hands it to NIKKO) And you, my dear, what an unexpected pleasure. It's so kind of you to visit me in my loneliness.*

1 ripe mango, peeled and sliced
2 ripe kiwis, peeled and sliced
2 tablespoons sugar
4 ounces (120 ml) Grand Marnier or other orange-flavored liqueur
1 bottle (750 ml) white wine

Put mango and kiwi slices in a pitcher. Add sugar and Grand Marnier. Stir, mashing gently with a wooden spoon. Let marinate 10 to 15 minutes. Add wine. Chill several hours before serving.

MAKES 8 SERVINGS.

CHAMPAGNE CRYSTAL BALL

DOROTHY: *I'm here in Oz, Auntie Em! I'm locked up in the Witch's castle . . . and I'm trying to get home to you, Auntie Em! (AUNT EM's face has begun to fade from the crystal, having made no sign of hearing DOROTHY.)*

1 ounce (30 ml) cranberry juice
½ ounce (15 ml) ginger-flavored liqueur
4 ounces (120 ml) chilled champagne

Pour cranberry juice and ginger liqueur into a chilled 6-ounce (180-ml) champagne flute. Add champagne and serve immediately.

MAKES 1 DRINK.

WINKIE WINE PUNCH

WINKIES: *(chanting as they march)*
O—Ee-Yah! Eoh—Ah!
O—Ee-Yah! Eoh—Ah!
O—Ee-Yah! Eoh—Ah!

1 bottle (750 ml) red wine
1½ cups (360 ml) pear juice
1½ cups (360 ml) orange juice
2 small oranges, sliced
2 to 4 tablespoons sugar to taste (depending on sweetness of wine)

Mix all ingredients in a large pitcher. Refrigerate 1 to 4 hours, until ready to serve. Serve in tall glasses filled with ice.

MAKES 8 SERVINGS.

SWEET MARGARET-ITA

Lorna Luft, Garland's daughter, told an interviewer about the challenge her mother had acting scared of the Wicked Witch: "In between takes, Margaret would serve tea to Mama, and they would laugh so hard that Margaret's green makeup would start to run into her cup of tea. Mama said every time she would have to cower at the Witch, all she could think about was this soiled, discolored green crumpet Margaret would give her with all the panache of a great lady—as if she were some kind of Technicolor Queen Victoria." (From John Fricke, Jay Scarfone, and William Stillman, The Wizard of Oz: The Official 50th Anniversary Pictorial History, Warner Books, 1989.)

2 ounces (60 ml) tequila
2 tablespoons Coco Lopez (cream of coconut)
1 ounce (30 ml) fresh lime juice
lime wedge

Fill a large glass with ice, add all the ingredients, and shake until well blended. Strain into a chilled cocktail glass. Garnish with lime wedge.

MAKES 1 DRINK.

WARM APPLE WITCH'S BREW

WITCH: And now, my beauties! . . . something with poison in it, I think; with poison in it, but attractive to the eye and soothing to the smell! Heh, hch, heh, heh, heh, heh!

16 ounces (480 ml) apple cider
1 tablespoon pickling spices or mulling spices
1 cinnamon stick, broken in half

3 black peppercorns
4 ounces (12 ml) applejack brandy (optional)

In a small saucepan, bring all ingredients except applejack to a boil. Simmer for 3 minutes. If adding brandy, pour 2 ounces (60 ml) into each mug while other ingredients are simmering. When ready to serve, strain hot cider into 2 mugs. Stir. Spices can also be wrapped in cheesecloth and then heated in cider so that straining is unnecessary.

MAKES 2 DRINKS.

RASPBERRY HOURGLASS

DOROTHY: Oh, hurry! Please, hurry! . . . The hourglass is almost empty!

2½ cups (600 ml) vodka
2 tablespoons honey
6 large strawberries, hulled and thinly sliced
25 raspberries
2 tablespoons Chambord liqueur
1 tablespoon sugar

In a small pitcher, mix vodka, honey, strawberries, and raspberries. Let marinate for 2 to 3 days in refrigerator. Strain mixture, reserving vodka and berries separately. Puree berries in blender or food processor. Strain to remove seeds. Add sugar and Chambord to strained puree. Chill 4 thin cocktail glasses. Into each chilled glass, pour 5 ounces (150 ml) reserved vodka. Spoon 1 tablespoon of purée into each filled glass.

MAKES 4 DRINKS.

I'M MELTING

WITCH: *Ohhh! you cursed brat! Look what you've done! I'm melting! Melting! Oh, what a world! What a world! Who would have thought a good little girl like you could destroy my beautiful wickedness!*

8 ounces (240 ml) water
1 ounce (30 ml) creme de cacao
1 ounce (30 ml) Irish cream liqueur
1 teaspoon cocoa powder
2 teaspoons sugar
1 heaping teaspoon instant coffee granules
1 scoop vanilla ice cream

Bring water to a boil. Meanwhile, mix creme de cacao, Irish cream, cocoa powder, sugar, and instant coffee in a 12-ounce (360-ml) mug. Add boiling water and stir until dissolved. Top with vanilla ice cream and serve immediately.

MAKES 1 DRINK.

★ HEAD COUNT ★

How many directors worked on *The Wizard of Oz* and who were they?
Four—Richard Thorpe, George Cukor, Victor Fleming, and King Vidor.

Organize a scavenger's hunt with items seen or mentioned in the movie, such as an hourglass, apples, an umbrella, a basket, a polka-dot dress, a broom, and so on.

WICKED MINT WITCH

DOROTHY: Please sir, we've done what you told us: we've brought you the broomstick of the Wicked Witch of the West. We melted her.
OZ'S VOICE: Oh, you liquidated her, eh? Very resourceful.

4 ounces (120 ml) bourbon
½ ounce (15 ml) creme de menthe
fresh mint sprig

Pour bourbon and creme de menthe into a cocktail glass filled with ice cubes. Stir and garnish with fresh mint leaves.

MAKES 1 DRINK.

Dessert in the Emerald City

CABBY AND CITIZENS:
In the Merry Old Land of Oz
We get up at twelve and start to work at one,
Take an hour for lunch, and then at two we're done,
Jolly good fun.

Toto's Triple Chocolate Bark

TOTO rushes into the clearing, barking furiously.
TIN MAN: Look! There's Toto! Where'd he come from?
SCARECROW: Why, don't you see? He's come to take us to
  Dorothy!

5 ounces (142 g) white chocolate
5 ounces (142 g) milk chocolate
5 ounces (142 g) semisweet or bittersweet chocolate
3 teaspoons vegetable oil
4 ounces or 1 cup (114 g) chopped pecans
4 ounces or 1 cup (114 g) dried cherries

In 3 small heatproof bowls, melt the 3 different chocolates separately
with 1 teaspoon of oil in each. Melt over a pan of barely simmering
water or in microwave on medium for 2 to 3 minutes. Stir each bowl of
chocolate until smooth. Line a cookie sheet or baking pan with waxed
paper. Pour all 3 different melted chocolates onto pan next to each
other. Spread chocolates to about ½ inch (13 mm) thick and swirl
chocolates together to create marbleized effect with the tip of a sharp
knife. Quickly, before chocolate begins to set, sprinkle surface evenly
with pecans and then cherries. Cover chocolate with another piece of
waxed paper and press gently and evenly across surface. Let cool in in
refrigerator or freezer until ready to serve. When ready to use, peel off
waxed paper and break into pieces.

NOTE: This recipe works best with good-quality chocolates.

★ HORSE POWDER ★

How was the Horse of a Different Color turned green, blue, orange, red, yellow, and violet?

Six white horses were sponged down with Jell-O powder, as paint was unacceptable to both the ASPCA and the animals. This, however, was a time-consuming process because in between shots the horses usually managed to lick off most of the Jell-O.

Horse of a Different Color Jell-O

2 3-ounce (170 g total) packages lime-flavored gelatin
1 3-ounce (85-g) package grape-flavored gelatin
¾ cup (155 g) sour cream

1 ripe banana, peeled and thinly sliced
1 8-ounce (227-g) can pineapple chunks, rinsed and drained

Prepare 1 package of lime gelatin according to package instructions for molding. Pour immediately into a 2-quart (2-liter) mold. Let cool in freezer while preparing the second layer. Prepare grape-flavored gelatin and pour over layer of lime gelatin when the lime gelatin is firm to the touch. Let cool in freezer to set the second layer.

Meanwhile, prepare the third layer. In a medium bowl, mix 1 package lime gelatin with 1¼ cups (300 ml) boiling water. Stir to dissolve. Stir in sour cream. Fold in fruit. Pour over set second layer. Let mold set in refrigerator for several hours or overnight. To unmold, run knife around edges. Dip bottom of mold in warm water for 30 seconds. Place plate on top of mold and turn over. Shake gently to unmold.

MAKES 12 SERVINGS.

Emerald City Pistachio Layer Cake

MERINGUE LAYERS

8 large egg whites

¾ cup (150 g) sugar

¾ cup (95 g) ground pistachio nuts, unsalted and preferably skinned

BUTTERCREAM

¾ cup (150 g) sugar

½ cup (120 ml) water

5 large egg yolks

1½ cups (340 g) butter, at room temperature

pinch salt

½ teaspoon almond extract

1 cup (127 g) ground pistachio nuts, unsalted and preferably skinned

To make meringue layers, preheat oven to 375°F (190°C). Butter and flour 3 9-inch (23-cm) round cake pans. Cut parchment or waxed paper to fit bottoms of pans. Fit them into pans, then butter and flour paper. Beat egg whites in a large bowl with an electric mixer until very frothy. Add sugar in a thin stream while continuously beating. Beat until stiff peaks form. Fold in ground pistachios with a spatula. Gently spread in prepared pans, smoothing the tops. Bake on middle rack of oven for about 35 minutes or until meringues are well browned. Cool on rack 5 minutes, then remove from pans and remove paper. Let cool completely.

To make buttercream, combine sugar and water in small saucepan over medium-high heat. Have egg yolks ready in medium bowl. When sugar syrup comes to a boil, start beating yolks with electric mixer. Let syrup boil 4 minutes. While continuously beating yolks with mixer, add syrup in a thin stream. Continue beating until mixture is very light and thick and has cooled. In a separate bowl, cream butter well. Pour in egg mixture a little at a time, beating well after each addition. When fully incorporated, add salt and almond extract, then fold in ¾ cup (95 g) pistachios.

Assemble cake by spreading a layer of butter cream over each layer of meringue and stacking the layers. Spread more buttercream around sides and top of cake and then press remaining pistachios around sides of cake. Refrigerate at least 2 hours or overnight. Let cake sit at room temperature 1 hour before serving.

MAKES 10 TO 12 SERVINGS.

Beautiful Blondies

BEAUTICIAN: *We can make a dimpled smile out of a frown.*
DOROTHY: *Can you even dye my eyes to match my gown?*
BEAUTICIAN: *Uh-huh.*
DOROTHY: *Jolly old town!*

1¼ cups (284 g) unsalted butter, at room temperature

1¼ cups (300 g) firmly packed light brown sugar

3 large eggs

1¾ cups (245 g) all-purpose flour

2 teaspoons baking soda

¼ teaspoon salt

1 cup (90 g) sweetened coconut flakes

½ cup (45 g) sliced blanched almonds

½ cup (65 g) chopped walnuts

9 ounces (255 g) white chocolate chunks

Grease a 9 x 13 x 2-inch (23 x 33 x 5-cm) pan. Preheat oven to 350°F (180°C). In a large mixing bowl, beat butter and light brown sugar until creamy. Add eggs and continue to beat until well blended. In a small bowl, stir together flour, baking soda, and salt. Add dry ingredients to butter mixture. Stir until incorporated. Fold in remaining ingredients and spread batter evenly in prepared pan. Bake for 30 to 35 minutes, until cake is golden brown. Let cool. Cut into 2-inch (5-cm) squares.

MAKES 24 SQUARES.

King of the Forest
Plum Upside-Down Cake

DOROTHY: *Your Majesty, if you were King*
You wouldn't be afraid of anything? . . .
What about a hippopotamus!
LION: *Why, I'd thrash him from top to bottomus.*
DOROTHY: *Supposin' you met an elephant!*
LION: *I'd wrap him up in cellophant.*

3 cups (600 g) sugar
½ cup (120 ml) water
1 teaspoon lemon juice
6 to 8 ripe plums, pitted and sliced ¼ inch (6 mm) thick
1 cup (227 g) unsalted butter
1 teaspoon vanilla extract
½ teaspoon ground nutmeg
4 large eggs, separated
1 cup (240 ml) heavy cream
10 ounces (1 cup/284 g) mascarpone cheese
2 cups (280 g) cake flour
½ teaspoon salt
2 teaspoons baking powder

Preheat oven to 350°F (180°C). Lightly butter a 9 x 11-inch (23 x 28-cm) glass baking dish. To make caramel, in a clean saucepan, combine 1½ cups (300 g) sugar, the water, and lemon juice. Cook over medium-high heat until syrup is a golden caramel brown. Watch it closely as it burns quickly. Carefully pour into baking dish and tilt dish, using potholders, until caramel covers bottom completely. Allow 5 minutes for caramel to harden somewhat, then line caramel with plum slices, leaving no spaces.

Cream butter with 1 cup (200 g) sugar in large mixing bowl with an electric mixer. Add vanilla and nutmeg and then egg yolks one by one. Beat in heavy cream and mascarpone. Sift in 1 cup (140 g) of cake flour, the salt, and baking powder. Beat slightly until combined. In a separate bowl, beat egg whites and ½ cup (100 g) sugar with clean mixer attachment until soft peaks form, then beat 30 seconds longer. Slide egg whites onto batter, then sift remaining cup of flour on top. Fold together with a spatula. Spoon batter into dish lined with caramel and plum slices. Put dish into a larger baking pan and fill baking pan with hot water until it comes halfway up sides of batter-filled dish. Bake for about 40 minutes or until paring knife or wooden pick comes out clean. Carefully remove from oven. Let cake stand at room temperature for 4 to 5 minutes, still in water bath. Then run a paring knife around edge of pan and invert onto serving platter.

MAKES 10 TO 12 SERVINGS.

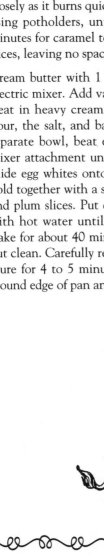

Chocolate Chip Macadamia Tart

WIZARD: Back where I come from, we have universities, seats of great learning—where men go to become great thinkers, and when they come out, they think deep thoughts—and with no more brains than you have—but! they have one thing you haven't got! A diploma.

TART CRUST
1½ cups (210 g) all-purpose flour
¼ cup (25 g) ground macadamia nuts
¼ cup (50 g) sugar
½ teaspoon salt
½ cup (114 g) cold unsalted butter, cut in ½-inch (13-mm) pieces
juice of 1 orange
3 tablespoons cold water

FILLING
3 large eggs
½ cup (100 g) sugar
grated zest or rind of 1 medium orange
½ cup (105 g) sour cream
1 cup (240 ml) heavy cream
¾ cup (95 g) coarsely chopped macadamia nuts
4 ounces (114 g) coarsely chopped bittersweet or semisweet chocolate

Preheat oven to 350°F (180°C). To make crust, combine first 4 ingredients in large bowl. Cut in butter pieces until mixture resembles coarse sand. Add orange juice and water and mix with hands until a dough is formed. Wrap in plastic or foil and refrigerate 15 minutes.

Roll out dough ¼ inch (6 mm) thick and fit into 9- or 10-inch (23- or 25-cm) buttered tart pan or quiche dish. Put in freezer for at least ½ hour. Weight tart shell with aluminum foil filled with raw rice, dried beans, or pie weights. Bake for ½ hour. Remove foil and bake 5 more minutes. Lower oven temperature to 325°F (165°C).

To make filling, in a medium bowl, whisk together eggs, sugar, and zest. Add sour cream and heavy cream and combine thoroughly. Sprinkle tart shell with ½ of nuts and chocolate pieces. Pour egg mixture into shell and then sprinkle top with remaining nuts and chocolate pieces. Bake 35 to 45 minutes or until custard is just set. Serve while still warm.

MAKES 8 TO 10 SERVINGS.

Stratospheric Mint Soufflé

WIZARD: *(with dignity) Child, you cut me to the quick! I'm an old Kansas man myself . . . born and bred in the heart of the Western wilderness, premier balloonist par excellence to the Miracle Wonderland Carnival Company—until one day, while performing spectacular feats of stratospheric skill never before attempted by civilized man, an unfortunate phenomena occurred. The balloon failed to return to the fair.*

1¼ cups (250 g) sugar

4 large eggs, separated

4 tablespoons (60 ml) peppermint schnapps

2 teaspoons mint extract

2 cups (480 ml) heavy cream

3 tablespoons (15 g) minced fresh mint

1 5¼-ounce (150-g) package European-style chocolate-topped butter cookies

Fit 10 individual 8-ounce (120-ml) soufflé dishes or a single 1-quart (1-liter) soufflé dish with foil collars that have been lightly oiled. Bring ¾ cup (180 ml) of the sugar and ½ cup (120 ml) water to a boil in a small saucepan. As soon as it starts to boil, begin beating egg yolks in a medium bowl with electric mixer. Boil sugar syrup 4 minutes. While continuously beating yolks, add sugar syrup in a thin stream. Beat yolks until they are cooled to room temperature. Beat in 2 tablespoons schnapps and 1 teaspoon mint extract. Refrigerate.

Make another syrup with ½ cup (100 g) sugar and ⅓ cup (80 ml) water. When it comes to a boil, start beating egg whites in separate clean bowl with a clean mixer attachment. Let syrup boil for 3 minutes. While continuously beating whites, carefully add syrup in a thin stream. Continue beating until a fairly stiff, shiny meringue forms. Set aside. Beat heavy cream with remaining 2 tablespoons of schnapps and 1 teaspoon of mint extract until soft peaks form. Stir in fresh mint.

Remove yolk mixture from refrigerator. Fold meringue into yolk mixture, then fold in whipped cream. Fill soufflé dishes with mixture. Freeze for at least 4 hours or overnight. Make coarse cookie crumbs from the chocolate-topped butter cookies by putting them in a food processor or chopping by hand. Remove soufflés from freezer 10 to 15 minutes before serving. Remove collars. Press cookie crumbs onto sides of soufflé and cover top with remaining crumbs.

MAKES 10 SERVINGS.

Courageous Chocolate Cheesecake

WIZARD: *Therefore, for meritorious conduct, extraordinary valor, conspicuous bravery against wicked witches, I award you the Triple Cross. You are now a member of the Legion of Courage.*

CRUST

2 cups (250 g) chocolate wafer crumbs (32 crumbled chocolate wafers)

6 tablespoons (85 g) unsalted butter, melted

FILLING

3 8-ounce (681-g) packages cream cheese, at room temperature

1½ cups (250 g) sugar

1 teaspoon vanilla extract

3 large eggs

8 ounces (227 g) semisweet chocolate, melted

6 ounces (170 g) white chocolate chips or chunks

melted white chocolate

melted dark chocolate

Preheat oven to 325°F (165°C). Grease a 9-inch (23-cm) springform pan. To make crust, in a medium mixing bowl, stir together crumbs and melted butter. Press crumbs onto bottom and sides of springform pan. To prepare filling, beat together cream cheese and sugar until creamy and free of lumps. Add vanilla and eggs, one at a time, beating after each addition. Stir in melted chocolate and then white chocolate chips. Pour into prepared crust. Wrap bottom of springform pan with aluminum foil (to prevent water from seeping in) and set in a larger pan. Fill larger pan with hot water until it comes halfway up sides of springform pan. Bake for 1 hour. Remove from oven and cool in pan with water. Chill in refrigerator several hours or overnight. Unmold cheesecake. Decorate with drizzles of melted white and dark chocolate.

MAKES 8 TO 10 SERVINGS.

Homeward Bound Berry Pear Crumble

DOROTHY: *...there's no place like home; there's no place like home...*

3 medium pears, peeled, cored, and thinly sliced
½ pint (227 g) raspberries
1 pint (454 g) blueberries, washed and stems removed
1 vanilla bean, split and seeds scraped out
juice of 1 lemon
½ cup (100 g) sugar

TOPPING
¾ cup (105 g) all-purpose flour
¾ cup (75 g) rolled oats
½ cup (120 g) firmly packed brown sugar
½ cup (114 g) unsalted butter, softened
½ teaspoon ground cinnamon
vanilla ice cream or whipped cream (optional)

Grease a 2½-quart (2.5-liter) baking dish. Preheat oven to 375°F (190°C). In a medium bowl, gently toss fruit with vanilla bean seeds, lemon juice, and sugar. Arrange evenly in baking dish. In a small bowl, stir together ingredients for topping. Sprinkle over top of fruit. Bake for about 30 minutes, until top is golden and pears are cooked. This is especially good served with vanilla ice cream or whipped cream.

MAKES 6 SERVINGS.